COLLABORATE BETTER

Based on *Collabor(h)ate* by Deb Mashek, PhD

First published in Great Britain by Practical Inspiration Publishing, 2025

© Deb Mashek and Practical Inspiration Publishing, 2025

The moral rights of the author have been asserted.

ISBN 978-1-78860-815-2 (paperback)
      978-1-78860-816-9 (ebook)

All rights reserved. This book, or any portion thereof, may not be reproduced without the express written permission of the publisher.

Every effort has been made to trace copyright holders and to obtain their permission for the use of copyright material. The publisher apologizes for any errors or omissions and would be grateful if notified of any corrections that should be incorporated in future reprints or editions of this book.

EU GPSR representative: LOGOS EUROPE, 9 rue Nicolas Poussin, LA ROCHELLE 17000, France Contact@logoseurope.eu.

Want to bulk-buy copies of this book for your team and colleagues? We can customize the content and co-brand *Collaborate Better* to suit your business's needs.

Please email info@practicalinspiration.com for more details.

Contents

Series introduction... iv
Introduction 1
Day 1: The realities of workplace collaboration........ 5
Day 2: The Mashek Matrix – understanding your collaborative relationships 21
Day 3: Assessing and improving relationship quality..34
Day 4: Understanding interdependence................... 45
Day 5: Diagnosing your collaboration issues.......... 56
Day 6: Fixing a broken collaboration........................ 67
Day 7: Better collaborative habits.............................. 75
Day 8: Knowing when (and how) to get the heck out.. 83
Day 9: Becoming a CollaborGREAT collaborator.... 94
Day 10: Creating a culture of effective collaboration 101
Conclusion 109
Endnotes 111

Series introduction

Welcome to *6-Minute Smarts*!

This is a series of very short books with one simple purpose: to introduce you to ideas that can make life and work better, and to give you time and space to think about how those ideas might apply to *your* life and work.

Each book introduces you to ten powerful ideas, but ideas on their own are useless – that's why each idea is followed by self-coaching questions to help you work out the 'so what?' for you in just six minutes of exploratory writing. What's exploratory writing? It's the kind of writing you do just for yourself, fast and free, without worrying what anyone else thinks. It's not just about getting ideas out of your head and onto paper where you can see them; it's about finding new connections and insights as you write. This is where the magic happens.

Whatever you're facing, there's a *6-Minute Smarts* book just for you. And once you've learned how to coach yourself through a new idea, you'll be smarter for life.

Find out more...

Introduction

The trailer park. My parents' alcoholism. My PhD. These were my three great teachers of collaboration.

I spent my childhood in a trailer park in western Nebraska. Summer days were spent outside, engaged in mixed-age, mixed-gender play. We turned the empty lots into restaurants, the trees into exclusive clubhouses and the asphalt grid on which the trailers rested into a play mat for ornate games of hide and seek.

The adults were largely absent; this was, after all, in the 1970s, before milk cartons broadcast missing children and before a culture of parental protectionism took hold. Us kids figured out on our own how to coordinate across interests, to set and enforce rules and to take care of each other along the way. Free-range play meant I had plenty of opportunity to build the social skills that I would later need to be an effective collaborator.

My parents' chronic alcoholism was a second great teacher for collaboration. As with so many kids who grow up amid addiction, home life was chaotic. Adults acted like children. Children acted like adults.

I learned to track and respond to others' needs and to figure out how to smooth over differences of opinion with grace. These interpersonal strategies – childhood superpowers, really – ensured that I could hold onto whatever threads of connection I could find. Often, that connection would come from caring adults outside my family. Teachers, youth group leaders and parents of friends. I learned to draw positive attention and affection from others by being useful, by being pleasant and by anticipating needs. Connecting with others meant they would provide what I craved most: security.

Now, as an adult, I've worked diligently in the therapy room and beyond to turn those default settings into deliberate decisions, choosing when to activate these powers while also recognizing – and voicing – my needs and wants along the way.

Thanks to an incredible high school guidance counsellor, I made it to college and from there to graduate school, where I discovered the psychology of close relationships.

I found the field fascinating. I had no idea a field of study existed in which scholars focused on

Introduction

understanding what makes relationships work, and I wanted to know what those scholars knew. I wanted to know what it takes to create the sort of healthy relationships I found utterly foreign and completely unprepared to pursue or realize.

So I dug in.

I've spent the past 25 years learning about the psychology of relationships and applying that knowledge to real world challenges like collaboration building.

Over the years, I've had many opportunities to collaborate, and the experiences have run the gamut. Some have been soul-nourishing, high-achieving, inspiring and efficient. Others have been frustrating, draining and unproductive.

I'd like to say that I approach collaboration first and foremost as a researcher, but that's not true. I approach collaboration first and foremost as a kid from the trailer park who figured out early on the power of relationships to realize possibilities. The wisdom I gained growing up became the object of my inquiry as a scholar. And that inquiry, in turn, became my lens for helping people who either need or want to work well with others.

I began developing frameworks and sharing them with others. First with students, then with colleagues, and eventually with nonprofit leaders, executives and cross-sector professionals. Over and over again, people told me the same thing: 'This changes how I think about working with others.'

This book exists to help you work with others. And, let's face it, collaboration is everywhere. And it's hard. And it's absolutely critical.

In our modern world, collaboration holds the key to solving the world's most complex problems. For both individuals and organizations, collaboration is – ironically – a competitive advantage, unlocking potential and driving progress.

Collaboration doesn't have to be a slog. I believe we can build skills, awareness and habits that make working together less painful and more powerful. We can – and should – do 'together' better.

Over the next ten chapters (ten days, if you fancy treating this as a mini course), you're going to discover ten key principles for better collaboration and experiment with using them for yourself.

Let's go!

Day 1
The realities of workplace collaboration

Many people move about the world with a vague sense that working together is a good thing – something we *should* do. Individuals strive to collaborate in their relationships, work lives and extracurriculars. Companies big and small proclaim collaboration a core value. A tennis shoe company teams up with a bag of potato chips to save the environment. Put a couple of smart people with good ideas on a project, the thinking goes, and you'll get lightning.

But what is collaboration, exactly?

Let me offer a definition:

> Collaboration is the process of two or more known individuals working together intentionally to advance a specific shared goal.

That definition gives us three key ingredients. First, the work must be *intentional*. Second, it must happen between *known* individuals. And third, it must advance a *specific shared goal*.

Being passionate about the same cause isn't collaboration. Working next to each other on separate things isn't collaboration. Even being on the same team doesn't necessarily mean you're collaborating. Collaboration requires *together work* – co-labouring with intention.

How common is collaboration in the workplace?

Based on this definition, I asked 1,100 people in the Workplace Collaboration survey what proportion of their job entails collaborating with others to advance shared goals. Keep in mind, this sample excluded 'lone rangers' – people who don't work with others.

Here's what they said when asked what proportion of their job entails collaborating with others to advance shared goals:

The realities of workplace collaboration

- 12% collaborate between 1–20% of the time
- 16%: 21–40%
- 24%: 41–60%
- 25%: 61–80%
- 22%: over 81% of the time.

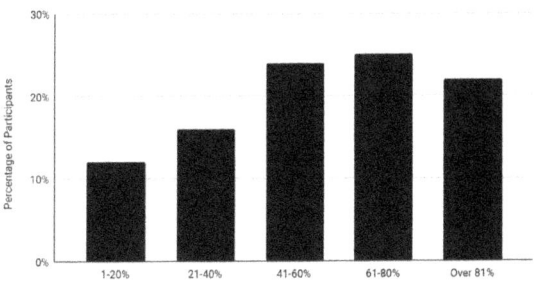

In other words, 71% of the sample reported spending at least 41% of their work life – that's over three hours per day in a 'typical' work day – collaborating with others. (When asked how much time they would *ideally* spend collaborating, 47% indicated they'd like to spend at least 41% of their time collaborating.)

People tended to have between two to five collaborations generally involving three to seven collaborators.[1] On average, people reported being involved in just under six collaborations. These collaborations typically involved just under six core collaborators.

Why is collaboration so common?

Workplace collaboration is common for at least three reasons.

First, and perhaps least interesting, the work itself is often embedded in complexity. Because no one person can know or do everything, collaboration among individuals, departments, divisions and even organizations is necessary to bring even relatively basic ideas to fruition. For example, if a trainer wants to host a guest speaker, they'll likely need involvement from Accounts Payable (to process payment), Communications (to design the promotional materials), IT (to provide access) and Facilities (to manage the room set-up). Collaboration is often required simply to navigate through the complexity of the workplace itself.

Second, and much more interesting, collaboration allows us to do more than we could on our own. It combines skill sets, perspectives and resources. Like a builder's team – carpenter, electrician, plumber, finisher – collaboration opens the toolbox wider. As one scientist I interviewed put it, the scope of the questions being asked in many fields, the varied arenas of knowledge that must be integrated to answer them and the availability of new technologies to explore them mean that 'science now requires a level of collaboration that has never happened before'.

Third, collaboration fuels innovation. Especially in cross-functional, skip-rank and demographically diverse teams, people generate more creative ideas and more effective solutions. Research shows that papers written by ethnically diverse teams are published in more prestigious journals and cited more often. In fields from business to law, demographically diverse teams make smarter decisions. Antonin Scalia, a conservative justice on the US Supreme Court, understood this, which is why he always hired at least one left-leaning clerk to balance his own perspective.

In short: collaboration makes the impossible possible. It's a competitive advantage.

What's at stake when collaboration sizzles — or fizzles?

When collaboration *sizzles*, everyone benefits.

You benefit: you learn, expand your network, gain visibility, grow professionally and have more fun at work.

Your team benefits: stronger engagement, more inclusive contributions and better solutions.

Your project benefits: more creativity, optimized priorities and better client experiences.

Your organization benefits: more effective resource use, better morale, stronger retention and a healthier bottom line.

But when collaboration *fizzles*?

You get stressed: your reputation suffers, your satisfaction tanks and your unique strengths go underutilized.

Your team gets mired: distrust emerges, communication breaks down and people withdraw.

Your project runs over budget or deadline: quality drops and clients get frustrated.

Your organization wastes crucial elements: time, money and talent – and people leave.

In summary, poor collaboration is a liability. When collaboration goes wrong, everything is at stake. As one business leader said to me, 'It follows you around like a cart full of bricks.'

Mixed feelings about collaboration? Welcome to the club

If your relationship with collaboration is complicated, you're not alone.

When I ask people to describe collaboration in three words, their responses are often mixed. They

The realities of workplace collaboration

say 'opportunity' and 'essential' in the same breath as 'frustrating' and 'scary'.

My findings back this up. In a College Pulse survey I ran with 500 college students:

- 49% felt *somewhat* or *very negative* about team projects
- Only 2% felt *very positive*.

In my Workplace Collaboration survey, the average rating for 'how do you feel about collaboration' was a decent 5.29 on a 7-point scale. Yet:

- 72% had experienced a collaboration that was 'absolutely horrendous'
- 85% had experienced one that was 'absolutely incredible'
- 63% had experienced *both*.

When I asked participants to rate their current collaborative relationships on a scale from 0 ('CollaborHATE') to 100 ('CollaborGREAT'), people used the whole scale. In other words, a whole lot of people out there have mixed feelings about collaboration. They know it is ripe with potential and that it can be incredibly rewarding. *And* they know it can also be an incredible burden, ripe with headache and heartache.

Despite all this, most people *want* to be good collaborators. Maybe because they value the principle, or maybe because they know their success depends on it.

But when people try to collaborate, they often unleash a Pandora's Box of messiness, complication and frustration. I want us to talk about that struggle. I want it to be acceptable to say out loud, 'Argh, this whole playing well with others thing is really difficult.'

Let's give voice to that ambivalence, because if we don't acknowledge it, we miss opportunities to improve. Understanding the interpersonal dynamics at play is the first step toward healthier, more sustainable collaboration.

Collaboration, why do I hate thee? Let me count the ways

I've identified 24 common ways collaboration goes sideways. Buckle up:

1. **Dropped balls**: Someone says they'll do something and doesn't.
2. **Uneven workload**: Some people carry the team; others coast.
3. **'My way or the highway'**: One person decides for the group.

The realities of workplace collaboration

4. **'I'll just do it myself'**: Someone decides it'll be quicker and simpler if they just do it.
5. **No capacity to give**: Someone volunteers but they're overcommitted already.
6. **Under preparation**: People turn up not ready to engage and slow everything down.
7. **Disengagement**: Emails go unanswered. Meetings become background noise.
8. **Herding cats**: Someone shoots off on their own, creating chaos and confusion.
9. **Too-late contributions**: Input arrives too late to be useful, but just in time to disrupt the work.
10. **Inconsistent contributions**: Someone's all in, then disappears only to reappear a week later.
11. **Stealing credit and placing blame**: One person takes all the credit/shirks the responsibility.
12. **Off-loading risk**: One party tries to snag all the upside and dodge all the downside.
13. **Egos, titles and credentials**: Someone focuses exclusively on their own needs and interests.
14. **Hoarding and withholding**: One person hoards access to information, insights, tools or people.

15. **Tyranny of perfectionism**: People refuse to share early-stage work, holding things up and creating an unhelpful high-stakes environment.
16. **Dodging hard conversations**: Avoiding differences of opinion makes it hard to talk about important issues.
17. **Mushy roles**: Poorly defined roles mean confusion and patchy coverage.
18. **Failing to decide how to decide**: When the decision-making process is unclear, it's a mess.
19. **Tool overload**: Everyone mindlessly imports their favourite tech tool, no one knows what's what or where key documents are.
20. **Asymmetrical power**: Power imbalances impede information flow and make accountability conversations difficult.
21. **Responsibility without authority**: It's your responsibility to get the project delivered, but the engineers don't report to you.
22. **Hiding**: Someone's stuck, but they keep quiet.
23. **Poisoned well**: The organizational culture is so toxic that trust, goodwill and care go out the window.
24. **Undermining**: Someone intentionally sabotages a colleague's work.

The realities of workplace collaboration

Gulp. That's a long list of ways collaboration can go off the rails. Frankly, these potholes along the road to collaboration aren't all that surprising given how few people ever receive any training in how to collaborate well.

Do we teach this stuff? Nope

Despite collaboration's importance, we rarely teach it.
In college:

- 65% of students said they received *no training* in how to collaborate
- 22% got only 'a few minutes'.

In business school:

'We throw them into groups and tell them to work together,' one professor admitted, 'but we don't actually give them any tools.'

In the workplace:

- 31% said they'd received *no professional development* in collaboration
- Only 26% had received 'more than a couple hours'.

Yet:

- 77% want to develop their collaboration skills
- 81% believe their success depends on them.

Collaboration is critically important. It's hard to do well, and yet there seems to be a general belief that this is a skill one can just pick up by osmosis via on-the-job training amid a bunch of other professionals who likewise haven't had any formal training. Like trying to construct an IKEA dresser without the instructions, everyone is feeling their way through the complexities. It's no wonder so many collaborative projects encounter snags, fall flat or result in good talent heading for the door. We can do better, but where shall we start?

Start with relationships

Collaboration is built on a trifecta: people, tools and processes. But it's the people who matter most.

As one nonprofit founder noted, 'Good people figure out how to get it done with the tools available to them, even if the tools are crappy… they find a way to get it done.'

The realities of workplace collaboration

Relationships make or break collaboration. That's where we begin.

Fear not, this is learnable

Just like being a good partner or parent, being a good collaborator is something you can learn. You don't have to rely on osmosis. It's possible to build healthier, more productive collaborative relationships – and to make collaboration not only more effective, but also more joyful.

I wish every person who ever works with other people – in other words, the overwhelming majority of the workforce – could benefit from professional development aimed at improving their collaborative relationships.

That's why I wrote this book.

So what? Over to you…

1. What adjectives best describe your feelings toward collaboration at work? Why?

The realities of workplace collaboration

2. Reflecting on your past collaborations, what pitfalls have you encountered? How might you address them more effectively next time?

3. In your current collaborations, where do you see the greatest need for relationship-building?

Day 2
The Mashek Matrix — understanding your collaborative relationships

Americans spend more time working than on all other waking activities combined.[2] And a whole lot of that time is spent collaborating. But here's the thing: just because we spend time working together doesn't mean we do it well. Nor does it mean we know what's actually going on in our relationships at work.

We often treat workplace relationships as background noise – as something that's 'just there'. But in truth, these relationships are critical.

When these relationships are strong, collaboration feels energizing and effective. When they're strained, collaboration becomes frustrating, inefficient or even impossible. It's no wonder that a study by Simpli5 found that '41.2% of respondents felt friction in collaboration, and nearly a third had considered quitting their job because of negative team dynamics'.[3]

That's why I developed something called the *Mashek Matrix*.

The two questions that matter most

Before we jump into the framework, I want to start with two deceptively simple questions:

1. How good is your relationship?
2. Do you and your collaborator influence each other's outcomes?

These questions form the heart of the Mashek Matrix.

Relationship quality: how good is your relationship?

Psychologists focused on close relationships define relationship quality as:

> 'A person's subjective perception that their relationship is relatively good versus bad.'

In other words, if you think your relationship rocks, then it counts as high quality. And that subjective assessment predicts all sorts of real-life outcomes. People in higher-quality relationships recover faster from injuries, live longer and experience fewer symptoms of depression and anxiety.

So what does *collaborative relationship quality* look like?

I define it as:

> Your subjective sense of how good or bad your relationship is with a particular collaborator.

It includes things like trust, satisfaction, commitment, self-expansion and excitement. While research suggests these are less distinct from each other in collaborative contexts than in romantic ones, they're still useful to keep in mind.

In the Workplace Collaboration survey, I found that higher relationship quality correlates with:

- Greater job satisfaction
- Fewer mental health symptoms
- More positive attitudes toward collaboration.

And these effects hold even when controlling for overall collaboration attitudes. In other words, even if you're not naturally a fan of teamwork, *being in high-quality collaborative relationships still makes your work life better.*

Your Collaborative Relationship Quality score maps onto the *vertical axis* of the Mashek Matrix.

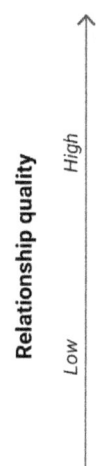

Figure 2.1: Collaborative relationship quality axis

Interdependence

Now let's talk about the second big idea: *interdependence*.

To define it, I'll borrow from Harold Kelley and colleagues, who asked a simple but profound question: 'What is a relationship?'

Their answer? Two people are in a relationship if their outcomes are interdependent – that is, if what one person does affects what the other experiences.[4]

The Mashek Matrix

Interdependence varies in three main ways:

1. **Frequency:** How often do you interact?
2. **Diversity:** In how many different domains do you influence each other?
3. **Strength:** How big is the impact of one person's behaviour on the other's outcomes?

Think of a student group project: if you divvy up the work, disappear and all come back just to staple the work together, that's *low* interdependence.

Contrast that with a workplace team that's tackling a messy problem with no obvious solution, where everyone's work affects everyone else's progress. That's *high* interdependence.

Interdependence can be a gift – or a nightmare. It enables deep collaboration, but it also means your work is no longer just your own. If your teammate drops the ball, *you* feel the pain. If their part runs late, *your* part stalls. If they do great work, *you* shine. But if things go sideways, *your* reputation, review metrics and sanity may be on the line.

Your interdependence score maps onto the *horizontal axis* of the Mashek Matrix.

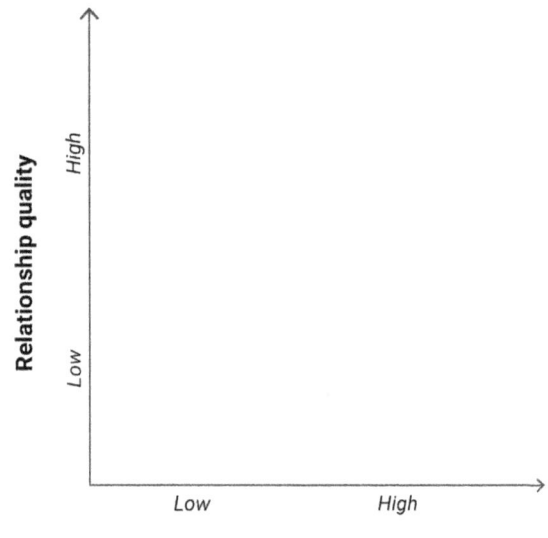

Figure 2.2: Interdependence axis

Introducing the Mashek Matrix

Now we put it all together.

The Mashek Matrix is a 2x2 model built on:

- **Vertical axis:** Collaborative Relationship Quality
- **Horizontal axis:** Interdependence.

Each axis ranges from low to high. That gives us four collaborative 'zones'.

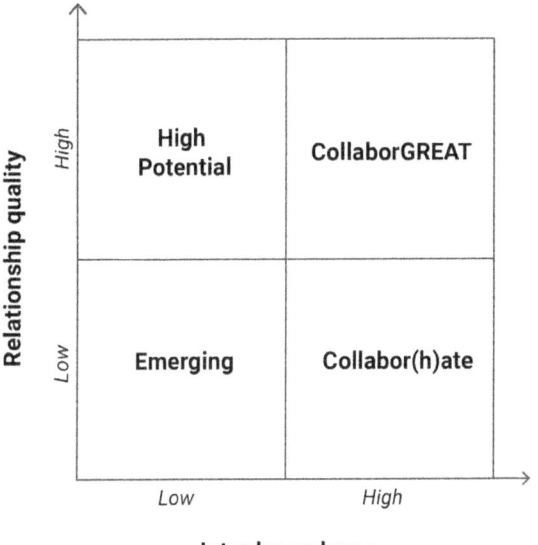

Figure 2.3: The Mashek Matrix

Let's explore them.

CollaborGREAT (high quality, high interdependence)

This is the sweet spot. You trust each other, enjoy working together and your success depends on shared outcomes. You're engaged, responsible and responsive. This is where deep collaboration happens – the kind where the work is better *because* you did it together.

When people in my research were asked to name the most *meaningful* person in their most important collaboration, they overwhelmingly chose collaborators in this quadrant.

High Potential (high quality, low interdependence)

This is a feel-good but underleveraged relationship. You get along well, but you're not relying on each other much. The relationship has a solid foundation – it's just not being tapped for its full potential. With more intentional structure or shared responsibilities, this can evolve into something powerful.

Emerging (low quality, low interdependence)

These relationships are… fine. Nothing special, nothing stressful. There's little connection and little overlap. The collaboration might be superficial or early stage. Think of this as 'meh-collaboration'. It's not draining, but it's not really delivering either.

Collabor(h)ate (low quality, high interdependence)

Welcome to the danger zone. You *need* each other to succeed – but you don't trust each other, don't enjoy the work and may even dread the next meeting. This is where collaboration feels like being hitched to a runaway horse.

And because of the high stakes and tight links, *you can't escape without cost*. These collaborations are profoundly stressful and often unsustainable.

Why the Matrix matters

The Matrix gives you language – and a strategy – for understanding your collaborative relationships.

Rather than thinking in binary terms (good versus bad, team player versus lone wolf), you can diagnose where things are and what needs to change. Maybe you have trust, but you're working in silos (High Potential). Maybe you're forced to depend on someone who constantly lets you down (Collabor(h)ate). Maybe your team has room to grow.

The key insight is this: collaborative *relationship quality and interdependence are independent*. You can move one without the other – and understanding that is the secret to building better collaboration.

We'll explore how to move along each axis in the next two chapters.

Here's the point

- Collaborative workplace relationships matter – both emotionally and practically.
- They vary in two key dimensions: relationship quality and interdependence.
- The Mashek Matrix maps these dimensions to reveal four common collaborative states.
- Understanding where you are is the first step to improving where you're headed.

The Mashek Matrix

 So what? Over to you...

1. Think of one of your workplace collaborations. Where do you think it falls on the Mashek Matrix?

2. In that relationship, what feels easier – building connection (quality) or deepening shared outcomes (interdependence)?

3. How might recognizing both dimensions help you be more strategic in shaping your collaborative relationships?

Day 3
Assessing and improving relationship quality

If we want to get better at collaboration, we need to look closely at the *relationships* it relies on. I'm not just talking about whether we get along, but something deeper – what researchers call relationship quality.

In the Mashek Matrix, which you met in Day 2, relationship quality forms the *vertical axis*. The higher up the axis, the better the relationship. Today, we're going to explore what makes a relationship 'high quality', why it matters for collaboration and what you can do if it needs improvement.

Assessing and improving relationship quality

What is relationship quality?

Scholars who study close relationships define relationship quality as a person's *subjective sense* that a relationship is relatively good versus bad. This applies to all kinds of relationships – romantic, familial and, yes, collaborative.

In romantic research, they often break it down into six components: trust, satisfaction, commitment, love, intimacy and passion. Obviously, workplace relationships don't need all six (and in most cases, definitely *shouldn't* include all six), but the first three – trust, satisfaction and commitment – are essential for collaboration.

Let's look at these in more detail.

Trust

Trust is about whether you believe your collaborator will do what they say they'll do. When trust is high, you don't have to double-check every action. When trust is low, you're constantly bracing for disappointment.

Satisfaction

Satisfaction refers to whether the relationship is *a source of good feelings*. Do you enjoy working with this person? Does your collaboration leave you energized – or depleted?

While we often treat job satisfaction as a product of compensation or workload, it's deeply tied to our working relationships. If you dread interactions with a teammate, it's hard to feel good about your day – even if you love the mission.

Commitment

Commitment reflects your sense that the relationship is worth maintaining over time. It's the intention to stay in it, even when it gets tough.

In workplace collaboration, commitment shows up when people are *willing to stay engaged*, even during rough patches. They don't ghost you when it gets hard. They show up prepared, respond to messages and follow through – not because someone's watching, but because they care about the shared work.

Assessing and improving relationship quality

Why relationship quality matters

High-quality collaborative relationships don't just feel good – they actually *produce better outcomes*.

As we saw on Day 1, there are many reasons why collaborations go sideways including misaligned expectations, missing trust or a lack of shared purpose. These relationship strains are common – but fixable. And these effects held even after controlling for general attitudes toward collaboration. That means *even people who don't love working in teams can have positive experiences if their relationships are strong*.

That's why we start here. If the relationship is frayed, the collaboration will suffer – no matter how brilliant the idea or well-designed the process.

Challenges to high-quality collaboration

Of course, not every relationship is great out of the gate. Here are a few of the challenges people describe in my interviews and surveys:

- Someone isn't pulling their weight
- Someone isn't showing up prepared
- One person is holding all the decision-making power
- Communication styles are misaligned

- Feedback is avoided, misunderstood or poorly delivered
- There's no shared sense of purpose.

These issues make the work harder – and the relationship worse. But most of them are fixable.

How to improve relationship quality

If you want to create high-quality, collaborative relationships – and if you're willing to put in a little work – here are nine strategies that research (and experience) show can help:

1. **Set clear expectations**: Expectations are the yardstick by which we judge whether things are going well or poorly. Clear expectations reduce confusion, increase accountability and improve the odds of collaboration going well. Don't assume alignment – have the conversation. Then revisit and revise expectations as the work evolves.
2. **Behave accordingly**: If you say you'll do it, do it. It's not enough to agree to expectations – you have to follow through. When people don't behave in line with expectations, trust erodes, backup systems emerge and collaboration gets a whole lot harder.

Assessing and improving relationship quality

3. **Avoid telling yourself stories:** When something feels off, it's easy to invent explanations. Our brains fill in missing information, and often not in charitable ways. Instead of assuming you know why someone acted a certain way, ask them. Stay curious.
4. **Embrace accountability:** When you realize you've dropped a ball or missed the mark, say something. Early and clearly. Owning mistakes builds trust. It shows your collaborator they can count on you – even when things don't go perfectly.
5. **Be responsive:** Responsiveness matters more than speed. You don't have to reply instantly, but you do need to show you're attuned. When someone reaches out, acknowledge it. Let them know you've heard them and when you'll follow up more fully.
6. **Bring the donuts:** Small acts of generosity build strong relationships. Offer help without being asked. Celebrate wins. Share resources. These micro-gestures matter.
7. **Do novel things together:** Trying new things together strengthens connection. Shared novelty promotes growth – what researchers

call 'self-expansion'. Even small switches in routine can re-energize a collaboration.
8. **Know your attachment orientation**: We all bring patterns from past relationships into our work lives. Some people cling. Some distance. Knowing your own tendencies – and noticing others' – can help you show up with more clarity, compassion and skill.
9. **Mind your personality**: Traits like agreeableness, conscientiousness and emotional stability affect collaboration. You don't have to overhaul your personality, but a little self-awareness goes a long way in building healthy, productive relationships.

Small shifts, big impact

You don't need to schedule a dozen 'relationship check-ins' to improve a working relationship. But small, intentional actions like these can transform a collaboration from strained to strong.

And even if the other person isn't doing these things yet, *you* can model the kind of relationship you want to build.

Assessing and improving relationship quality

When to let go

Not every relationship is worth saving. Sometimes, despite your best efforts, the other person doesn't engage, doesn't improve or doesn't care. In those cases, it's okay to step back – or, when possible, to *get out*.

We'll talk more about when and how to exit a collaboration later. For now, remember this: *you don't have to fix everything*. But you *do* have the power to change how you show up – and that can change a lot.

The bottom line

Strong collaborative relationships are built on trust, satisfaction and commitment. These aren't mysterious traits – they're patterns of behaviour. You can build them, bit by bit.

And when you do, you'll not only get better results – you'll actually *enjoy* working with others.

So what? Over to you…

1. Which of the nine relationship-building strategies comes most naturally to you? Which feels most challenging?

Assessing and improving relationship quality

2. Think about a strained workplace relationship you've experienced. Which strategy might have helped strengthen it?

3. How might being more mindful of your own personality and attachment tendencies improve your future collaborations?

Day 4
Understanding interdependence

Like any relationship, collaborative relationships vary in their degree of interdependence. The more frequent the interaction, the more interdependent the relationship. The wider array of activities influenced, the more interdependent the relationship. The stronger the influence, the more interdependent the relationship.

On the low end, you might see the 'divide and conquer' strategy. Students huddle for 15 minutes after class, decide who will prepare which section of the presentation, and then barely talk again until the night before when everyone dumps their slides together. Workplace parallels exist: one person writes copy, another does layout, another plans distribution. Divide and conquer.

In contrast, some collaborations are intensely interdependent. Your ability to fulfil your responsibilities depends on the work of others. Your risks and rewards are contingent on what other people do, or don't do. You share turf, talent, time and treasure and are likely optimizing across competing demands and navigating complexity along the way. This interdependence is both a blessing and a curse. It enables deep collaboration – we truly are able to do together that which none of us could have possibly done alone. But it also means that your work, and the consequences you experience because of that work, becomes profoundly tied to the actions of others on the team. Gulp.

This means others have a say in what we do and how we do it, and this can be experienced as a psychologically distressing threat to our autonomy. Interdependence opens up the possibility of getting burned. Big time.

And yet, if we want to realize the powerful potential afforded by deep collaboration, interdependence is essential.

In Day 3 we looked at ways to improve relationship quality; you're unlikely ever to want to intentionally reduce it.

Understanding interdependence

The same isn't true of interdependence. To progress through the Mashek Matrix, you'll need to adjust interdependence both up and down.

For example, if you're in a state of Collabor(h)ate, first focus on decreasing interdependence, not increasing quality. This might feel counterintuitive but think of it like working on a marriage: sometimes you just need some breathing room before you're ready for the hard work of improving relationship quality.

There are three ways to adjust interdependence, upwards or downwards: frequency, diversity and strength.

Four strategies to turn the frequency dial

1. **Change formal time together**: A second short meeting each week would help keep the forward momentum. Are others open to that? Would others be open to stepping back to an every-other-week meeting cadence? A similar shift could occur with side-by-side work time. Increasing or decreasing the frequency of such time together may shift how interdependent collaborators feel.

2. **Change informal time together**: Ask a colleague to join for a 'walk and talk' around the building. Grab coffee or lunch together. Pop into their office. Stop by their desk. Direct message them when you notice they're online. Alternatively, to reduce interdependence, put on noise-cancelling headphones, flip the sign on your door to 'do not disturb', block calendar time to protect your workflow and agree to save non-urgent items for standing meetings.
3. **Change how much headspace you share**: If you find yourself ruminating on something your colleague said or did – or failed to say or do – you're spending psychological time with them. That interdependence persists even if they're not in the room. Strategies like journalling, mindfulness, exercise and direct communication can help free up that bandwidth. To increase interdependence, consider reflecting on what you're grateful for in your colleague.
4. **Change expectations about response time**: Do we all agree to reply to questions posed to the group within two hours? Two days? Set a standard that will work with everyone's existing commitments and with cultural

norms within your organization, if relevant. Don't leave your team hanging: honour what the group decides.

One strategy to turn the diversity dial

Do more or less together

More interdependence is also possible when you engage in an increasingly diverse range of activities with your collaborator, and you can decrease interdependence by finding ways to do less together. That sounds straightforward but it isn't always easy, given all the constraints in a typical workplace. The work still needs to get done, right?

If you want to dial down your interdependence with a colleague, you could try asking your manager something like this: 'Collaborating on Project A instead of B would give me a stretch opportunity to demonstrate I'm ready for the next role up.'

Or if it's more interdependence you're after, you could try something like this: 'Taking up X role on Y project would help me put recent training into practice and cement that new learning.'

Five strategies to turn the strength dial

There are five strategies to adjust the *strength* of interdependence. The first two focus on how the work is structured. The last three concern how work is measured and rewarded.

1. Change how workflows are structured

Work can be designed so that collaborators must rely on one another for access to critical resources and so that completion of the work requires coordinated action. For example, the type of coordination matters:

- In **pooled** interdependence, individuals work separately and combine outcomes at the end
- In **sequential** interdependence, the output of one becomes the input for the next
- In **reciprocal** interdependence, all must work in back-and-forth fashion to complete tasks.

The greater the need to coordinate action and rely on others, the greater the interdependence.

Understanding interdependence

2. Change how resources are accessed

When only one person can access a needed file, tool or source of knowledge, others must rely on that person. When collaborators jointly access those resources – or when they must coordinate around how and when to access them – interdependence increases. Shared resource management can heighten interdependence.

3. Change how goals are specified

Goal structure matters. When each person on a team has *individual goals*, they are largely working alone, even if under the banner of collaboration. But when collaborators are assigned *shared group goals*, they become collectively responsible for achieving the desired outcome. This shifts the dynamic from 'my part' to 'our success'.

Goals can be specified at the level of the individual contributor or the level of the group. Imagine a fundraising team at a nonprofit organization has the goal to raise $10 million from new donors this year. The development manager has a choice to make here. They could specify that each of the five team members is expected to independently raise $2 million; this is an example of an individual-level goal. Or they could specify that the team as a whole is expected to raise $10 million; this is an example of a group-level goal. Group-level goals strengthen interdependence, whereas individual-level goals weaken it.

4. Change how progress is tracked

Measurement signals what matters. If only individual progress is tracked and reported, then that's what collaborators will focus on. But if only *team-level progress* is visible – such as when a dashboard displays group performance – joint ownership of the work is reinforced.

5. Change how rewards and costs are allocated

Consider how success is rewarded – and failure penalized. If each person is evaluated and compensated individually, they may prioritize their own performance, even at the expense of the group. But if *rewards and consequences are shared*, such as team-based bonuses or mutual performance reviews, collaborators are incentivized to support one another and ensure group success. Shared risk and reward fosters deeper interdependence.

Collaborative relationships vary in both quality and interdependence. In the Mashek Matrix,

Understanding interdependence

interdependence is the horizontal axis. The more collaborators are intertwined – via frequency, diversity and strength – the farther to the right they move on this axis. When combined with high relationship quality, this creates CollaborGREAT relationships. When interdependence is high but relationship quality is low, the result is Collabor(h)ate.

 So what? Over to you...

1. In one of your current collaborations, would dialling interdependence up or down improve the work?

2. How comfortable are you with shared responsibility?

Understanding interdependence

3. What small adjustment in frequency, diversity or strength could strengthen a key collaboration?

Day 5
Diagnosing your collaboration issues

Collaboration can be exhilarating – or exhausting.

While collaboration enables remarkable outcomes, many working relationships falter due to specific, recurring issues.

Back in Day 1 we looked at some of the most damaging patterns, such as dropped balls, uneven workloads, asymmetrical power, hiding problems and so on (go and remind yourself, if you can bear it). But these collaboration problems often reflect system-level issues, not just personal failings. Tool overload isn't about laziness; it's about systems gone awry. Responsibility without authority isn't personal weakness; it's a structural flaw. So recognizing these

Diagnosing your collaboration issues

patterns early can make the difference between small course corrections and catastrophic failure.

Looking at the system – not just the symptoms – helps pinpoint what's really going wrong.

That's where the Mashek Matrix can help. It gives you a way to map where things stand – and where they might be getting stuck. The Matrix is built on two independent dimensions: Collaborative Relationship Quality (vertical axis) and Interdependence (horizontal axis).

Together, these axes give rise to four types of collaborative experiences:

- **Collabor(h)ate** (low relationship quality, high interdependence)
- **Emerging** (low relationship quality, low interdependence)
- **High Potential** (high relationship quality, low interdependence)
- **CollaborGREAT** (high relationship quality, high interdependence)

Let's start with the one that tends to generate the most frustration: Collabor(h)ate. This is like having your wagon hitched to somebody else's unpredictable and ill-mannered horse. In this situation, people are at the mercy of teammates whom they don't trust, don't like and don't want to invest anything extra in.

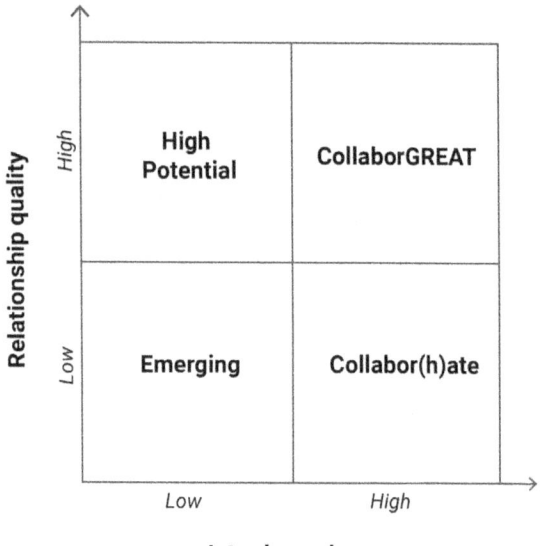

Figure 5.1: The Mashek Matrix

These relationships are incredibly stressful. And we want out.

But you can't always get out. You may still need to get the work done. So instead, you double-check everything. You avoid unnecessary interaction. You stew over unresolved tensions. The work continues, but the emotional toll is high.

Diagnosing your collaboration issues

Now contrast that with the Emerging quadrant. These collaborations aren't toxic – they're just not relationships yet. The work is likely superficial and intermittent. You may be coordinating on a surface level. Maybe you don't even know your collaborator's name. There's little connection, little overlap and little effort to change either.

Then there's High Potential. Here, the relationship quality is high, but the interdependence is low. You like and respect each other, but your work isn't really integrated. People enjoy being in the hopper together, but the co-labour – the together work – is likely more superficial than it could be given the strength of the relationship. These collaborations are underleveraged.

And finally, CollaborGREAT. This is the sweet spot. People are engaged. They're doing A+ work. They feel connected to each other and behave accordingly. They make the effort to see and be responsive to the needs of others. This combination of high relationship quality and high interdependence enables deep collaboration. We truly are able to do together that which none of us could have possibly done alone.

As we saw in Day 2, in my Workplace Collaboration survey, when participants were asked to name the most meaningful person in their most important collaboration, they overwhelmingly chose collaborators in the CollaborGREAT quadrant.

Plotting where your collaboration sits on the Matrix reveals not just what's wrong, but what type of solution might help. When you diagnose the systemic issues, you can more easily identify the actions that will address their root causes. And one set of issues you need to be particularly aware of – in others and in yourself – are the four collaboration killers.

Collaboration killers

In his classic book *The Seven Principles for Making Marriage Work*, relationship therapist John Gottman identified what he calls the 'four horsemen of the apocalypse', the behaviours that most reliably predict divorce. They are criticism, contempt, defensiveness and stonewalling:

- **Criticism**: In contrast to complaints, which concern someone violating a specific expectation or agreement, criticisms are global, negative assertions about another person.
- **Contempt**: Contempt, which can take the form of sarcasm, cynicism, name-calling, eye-rolling, mockery, hostile humour, belligerence

Diagnosing your collaboration issues

and sneering, signal disrespect and a sense of superiority over the other person.
- **Defensiveness**: Providing reasons or excuses that amount to blaming the other person or otherwise framing your own role as the innocent victim.
- **Stonewalling**: Withdrawing by falling silent, tuning out and withholding eye contact and other signals of presence.

These behaviours are bad news in any relationship, including your relationships with collaborators. While I'm unaware of any research that uses Gottman's argument-coding procedure to predict team distress and dissolution, I'd bet good money that the presence of these same four horsemen spell doom for collaborations.

If you notice yourself or others in your workplace exhibiting criticism, contempt, defensiveness or stonewalling, it's likely that without prompt and deliberate intervention, these relationships are likely headed for doom.

When it's clear things won't change

The Serenity Prayer, written by American theologian Reinhold Neibuhr and embraced by 12-step recovery programmes the world over, advises us to accept the things we cannot change, have the courage to change the things we can, and the wisdom to know the difference.

It also applies to the realm of workplace collaboration. Collaborations require care and intentionality, whether trying to establish first foundations or working to repair strained structures. Like all relationships, they take work.

You may personally be doing all the right things. You may have been more deliberate and persistent in your relationship-building efforts than in any other time of your career. And yet the collaboration or your relationships with your collaborators may nevertheless be fraught with struggle and disappointment.

There comes a time when you realize that, even though you have done everything you can reasonably do to get a troubled collaboration back on track, it remains unfulfilling, unproductive or unsustainable. A colleague may persist in their sabotaging behaviour. The team may be unable to walk the walk of their shared expectations. The organization may be unable or unwilling to change in light of feedback. As one HR professional told me,

Diagnosing your collaboration issues

'It doesn't matter a bit if you survey people but then don't do anything with the feedback – it's not enough to conduct a rinse and repeat survey once or twice a year because doing that alone doesn't create change. To create change you must reflect on what people say isn't working and be willing to do things differently going forward.'

When the juice is no longer worth the squeeze, accept the things you cannot change.

Then decide what action you'd like to take, realizing that inaction is also an option. Over the next few days we'll look at ways of fixing and maintaining relationships, but also at how to get the heck out if and when necessary.

So what? Over to you...

1. Reflect on a collaboration you're involved in: What systemic issues might be contributing to its challenges?

Diagnosing your collaboration issues

2. Which collaboration killer do you recognize in yourself?

3. What would it mean to accept that there are some aspects of a collaboration that you CAN'T change?

Day 6
Fixing a broken collaboration

As we've established, collaborations don't always go as planned. They drift. They stall. They sour. Whether you're stuck in Collabor(h)ate or simply want to make a good collaboration even better, this chapter gives you a step-by-step process for improving your relationships at work.

Once you've used the Mashek Matrix to help you understand where your collaboration stands now and what kind of relationship would better serve the work and the people involved, you can follow a nine-step process to support intentional, thoughtful improvement. These steps are based on research, refined through client experience and designed to be flexible. You can adapt, repeat, skip or reorder them as your situation demands.

Fixing a broken collaboration

Step 1: Find your current location

To get to where you want to be, first figure out where you are. Use the Mashek Matrix to map your current relationship on two dimensions: relationship quality and interdependence. You can assess intuitively or use the Collaborative Relationship Assessment available from my website.[5] Plot your current location as a dot and record the date.

Step 2: Identify your desired location

Next, determine where you'd like the collaboration to go. Your goal might be to move from Collabor(h)ate to CollaborGREAT – or just from Emerging to High Potential. Plot this target as a circle on the same Matrix. Make a note about why this destination matters to you right now.

Step 3: Determine the first step along the path

The route you take depends on your starting point. If you're in Collabor(h)ate (low relationship quality, high interdependence), the first step is to reduce interdependence. Trying to improve relationship

Fixing a broken collaboration

quality while tightly entangled often backfires. Instead, give the relationship breathing room so that mutual influence isn't overwhelming.

It's like a couple in crisis choosing to live apart for a while before diving into deep repair. Less entanglement gives space to rebuild quality. Then, and only then, increase interdependence again.

Step 4: Decide your preferred level of intervention

You have options. Change can begin:

- **Intrapersonally**: Shifting your mindset or behaviour
- **Interpersonally**: Engaging the other person directly
- **Structurally**: Changing norms, roles or systems
- **Team-wide or organizationally**: If the collaboration is embedded in bigger dysfunction.

Choose your lane based on power, trust and feasibility. Sometimes starting with yourself is best. Sometimes a broader change is needed.

Step 5: Brainstorm specific ideas

Now, generate a list of possible moves. If you want to increase quality, you might try expressing appreciation, asking thoughtful questions or showing up reliably. To deepen interdependence, try aligning goals or syncing schedules. Don't censor yourself – get creative.

Step 6: Systematically evaluate options

Look at each idea and ask:

- Is it feasible?
- Is it safe?
- Is it potentially effective?

Narrow your list to one or two promising options. Trust your instincts – but be strategic.

Step 7: Plan and implement

Pick your intervention. Plan when and how you'll do it. Aim for the smallest version of the change that still has 'teeth'. This is an experiment: 'If I try this, will the collaboration improve?'

Step 8: Observe and learn

Pay attention to what happens. Did the relationship shift? Did the work feel different? Were there ripple effects – positive or negative? Even if your effort doesn't yield success, you've gathered useful data.

Step 9: Now what?

Repeat the cycle. Try something else. Double down on what worked. Decide if the collaboration needs further improvement – or if you've arrived at a good-enough state. In some cases, the best move is to walk away. But often, small changes can unlock real momentum.

Here's the point

Relationship repair is a process. Start by understanding where you are. Clarify where you want to be. Then take small, purposeful steps in that direction. Even modest shifts in behaviour, mindset or structure can dramatically improve collaboration.

So what? Over to you...

1. Think of a struggling collaboration: Would it benefit more from strengthening relationships or deepening interdependence?

Fixing a broken collaboration

2. What is one low-key, moderate or full-on intervention you could implement this week?

3. What signals will you look for to find out if your small changes are improving the collaboration?

Day 7
Better collaborative habits

Collaborations don't flourish because of grand gestures. They thrive because of consistent, intentional habits. Small changes in how we communicate, navigate conflict and clarify expectations can dramatically improve how people feel in – and what they get out of – their collaborative relationships.

The power of communication

One strategy for building collaborative relationship quality is to improve communication. When people show up reliably – when they do what they said they'd do, respond to messages in a timely fashion and proactively update others on progress – it builds trust.

When they share early versions of their work so others can weigh in, listen actively and ask thoughtful questions, it signals care and respect.

Want to practise this strategy? Try saying something like, 'This is still half-baked, but I'd love your input' or 'Can you say more about that?' These statements help others feel seen and valued. That, in turn, builds relationship quality.

When someone feels their worth is contingent on presenting only perfect work, they sometimes keep collaborators at arm's length when developing work. Rather than seeking and getting constructive input on half-baked work early in its development, they wait until their piece is as perfect as possible before sharing it, making it difficult for others to contribute and creating a high-stakes environment where feedback can set back timelines or set off emotions.

Overcoming conflict and fostering psychological safety

Despite the importance of constructive tension in helping teams identify the best path forward, a conflict-averse member of the team may sweep differences of opinion aside, making it difficult for the team to optimize across competing demands.

Such behaviours can make it impossible to talk about important issues.

Establishing psychological safety is key. As defined by Harvard's Amy Edmondson, psychological safety is 'a shared belief held by members of a team that the team is safe for interpersonal risk taking'. When people experience psychological safety, they're more likely to share ideas, ask for help and admit mistakes.

You can help create this kind of safety by modelling vulnerability and appreciation. Say thank you when someone raises a hard issue. Acknowledge your own uncertainty. Make it clear that input is welcome – even when it challenges your ideas.

It helps to set expectations for how you'll handle disagreement. Decide together how to raise concerns, how to give feedback and how to reset when things go sideways. Naming these things up front helps everyone stay engaged when tensions rise.

Setting clear expectations and roles

Poorly defined roles result in confusion, redundant effort, absent talents and incomplete coverage.

Nobody can really explain how decisions are made, resulting in varied expectations and inevitably hurt feelings when people later feel cut out from decision making or burdened by decisions they'd rather not make.

Instead, decide how you'll decide. Will you aim for consensus? Appoint a decider? Use a voting system?

Clarify roles. Who's doing what? Who's responsible for delivering which pieces? Who needs to be consulted, informed or left alone?

The tool doesn't matter as much as the clarity. Use a RACI chart (a responsibility assignment matrix) or a team charter if that's helpful. Just make sure you get aligned about responsibilities and processes.

Better habits, better collaboration

Anything that would be a problem in any other kind of relationship will be a problem in a workplace setting; anything that will throw off a relationship will throw off a collaboration.

That includes avoiding conflict, hoarding information or failing to follow through.

The good news? These habits can be changed. Better communication. Clearer expectations. More safety and trust. These small shifts make a big difference.

Building new habits: start small and iterate

Forming better collaborative habits is not about overnight transformation.

Start small:

- Pick one or two habits to focus on at a time
- Anchor new habits to existing rhythms ('At the end of every meeting, we each name our next action')
- Celebrate small wins to reinforce new patterns.

It takes conscious effort at first.

Over time, new habits weave themselves into the relationship's fabric, until they feel effortless.

The pay-off of better habits

Better collaborative habits reduce stress, prevent conflict and create the conditions for real trust, creativity and high performance.

Instead of collaboration feeling like a source of friction, it becomes a source of flow.

Collaborators don't just tolerate each other – they enjoy building together.

Collaborate Better

You don't have to wait for others to change. You can start cultivating better habits in your collaborations right now.

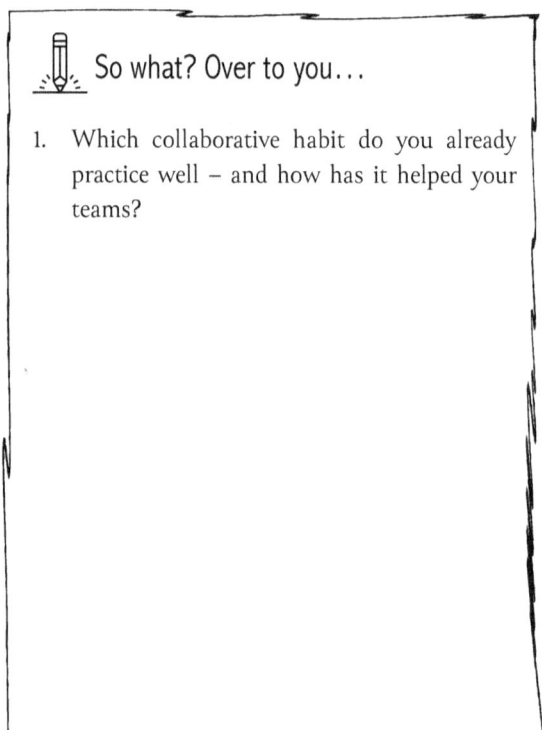

So what? Over to you...

1. Which collaborative habit do you already practice well – and how has it helped your teams?

Better collaborative habits

2. Which habit, if strengthened, would most improve one of your current collaborations?

3. What is one small, specific habit you could start this week to build stronger collaborative trust?

Day 8
Knowing when (and how) to get the heck out

Even when you enter a collaboration with the best intentions, the best collaborators and the best plans, sometimes things just don't work out. Collaborations can – and often do – end. Sometimes, exiting is the right call.

But how do you know when it's time to get the heck out? And if you do decide to leave, how do you do it well?

Let's start with the first question.

Recognizing when it's time to leave

Some collaborations are salvageable with effort and goodwill. Others, though, are beyond repair – or are simply no longer a good fit. Here are some indicators that it might be time to walk away:

- **The collaboration no longer serves the shared goal.** If the purpose that initially brought you together has shifted, disappeared or become irrelevant, it may be time to exit.
- **Trust has been irreparably broken.** Small betrayals may be repaired, but consistent violations of trust are a flashing red light.
- **There's a persistent mismatch in values.** If your core values are fundamentally out of sync with your collaborator's, it's going to be a rough road.
- **Power imbalances are being abused.** When one person consistently undermines, steamrolls or disregards another, that's a serious problem.
- **Communication patterns have broken down.** If communication is consistently toxic, absent or misaligned – and efforts to repair it have failed – continuing may do more harm than good.

Knowing when (and how) to get the heck out

- **The emotional toll is too high.** When a collaboration begins to sap your energy, damage your mental health or erode your sense of self, it's a sign that something needs to change.

Giving yourself permission to walk away

Leaving a collaboration can feel like failure. It can stir up guilt, fear and self-doubt. But exiting isn't necessarily a betrayal. Sometimes, it's the wisest, most courageous move you can make.

In my consulting work, I've seen people stay in damaging collaborations far too long because they felt obligated to 'make it work'. They worried about what others would think. They worried about burning bridges. They worried about hurting feelings.

Giving yourself permission to leave means honouring your needs, your values and your well-being. It means trusting that exiting can be an act of integrity, not just for you but for the collaboration itself.

How to exit well

Leaving is one thing. Leaving well is another.

If you do decide it's time to go, here are some guidelines to help you exit with integrity.

1. Communicate directly – and early

Don't ghost your collaborators. Don't quietly disengage and hope no one notices. Have a direct, respectful conversation about your decision.

Explain your reasons honestly but tactfully. Focus on your experience rather than blaming others.

Example:

- **Not this:** 'You're impossible to work with.'
- **Better:** 'I'm realizing that I'm not able to contribute to this collaboration in the way I'd hoped.'

2. Honour what you've accomplished together

Even if the collaboration ends on a difficult note, take time to recognize the good. What did you build together? What did you learn? What relationships were strengthened along the way?

Offering genuine appreciation helps preserve dignity on all sides.

3. Protect reputations

Resist the temptation to bad-mouth your collaborators after you leave. Speak well of people wherever you can. If you need to give honest feedback (for example, in an exit interview), do it privately and constructively.

Your professionalism in how you leave says as much about you as anything you did during the collaboration itself.

4. Reflect and learn

Every collaboration offers lessons. Successful or not, it gives you data for the future.

Ask yourself:

- What worked in this collaboration?
- What didn't?
- Where did I thrive?
- Where did I struggle?
- What will I do differently next time?

When you leave thoughtfully, you leave stronger.

While there's no one-size-fits-all script for breaking up with a collaborator, if you need to leave a collaboration, or to ask someone else to leave, these seven guidelines can help you do so in a way that is both direct and kind.

Collaborate Better

Guideline 1. As much as possible, while still doing what you need to get done, work to minimize the other's costs and maximize their benefits.

Guideline 2. Say what you mean; mean what you say. Be direct. Don't tuck the true meaning of your words behind mushy language.

Guideline 3. Be respectful. It goes without saying, but avoid name-calling, belittling, accusations, eye-rolling, jabbing comments, and so on.

Guideline 4. Have the conversation face-to-face (whether in-person or via video call) rather than via email. Sure, many of us feel more nervous about having a tough conversation face-to-face rather than sending a carefully crafted email. But, because it's so easy to misread what's in the written word and next to impossible to make space for others' reactions, the brave approach is the right approach if the goal is to dissolve the relationship gracefully and in a way that maximizes outcomes.

Guideline 5. Be brief. Say what you need to say in just a minute or two.

Knowing when (and how) to get the heck out

Guideline 6. Make space for the other person to say whatever they want to say, though resist engaging in debate, rebuttal, position defending and so on.

Guideline 7. Behave in a way you'll feel good about both now and in the future when looking back on this moment.

With those guidelines in mind, here's a template of key talking points. Keep your comments brief. Get in. Get out. Get on with it.

- **Say what the conversation is about.** It's amazing how often this important point is skipped in all sorts of break-up conversations, which leaves the listener asking, 'Wait: Are you breaking up with me?' If that's what you're doing, say so.
- **Point to the disconnect** between your needs (or the needs of your organization) and the realities of the collaboration.
- **Say directly** what you have decided.
- **Affirm your commitment** to a graceful transition.
- **Propose a follow-up conversation** over the next few days to co-create the transition plan.
- **Follow up** with an email.

Making peace with endings

If a collaboration isn't serving your needs, there's a reasonable chance the ending of that relationship will mean new growth opportunities for you, your organization and perhaps even your collaborator.

For example, you might now have time to invest in another promising partnership. Or to allocate more resources to another project that would benefit from your focused attention. In addition, you can reflect intentionally on the growth experienced because of the relationship.

These are all potential sources of growth from the collaboration that you get to take with you, even when the relationship ends. The trick is to be alert to the possibility of such growth and intentional about leveraging it.

Knowing when (and how) to get the heck out

✏️ So what? Over to you...

1. What signs have I seen (or ignored) in past collaborations that indicated it was time to exit?

2. When have I exited a collaboration well – and when have I handled it poorly? What made the difference?

Knowing when (and how) to get the heck out

3. How might I approach future collaboration exits with more integrity, clarity and care?

Day 9
Becoming a CollaborGREAT collaborator

You're here because you care about doing collaboration well. That starts with being thoughtful about what you say yes to – and how you show up once you've said it.

Just because you can collaborate doesn't mean you always should. I've had to learn this the hard way.

When people ask me to join a collaboration, I run it through four questions:

- Does it align with my values?
- Can I meaningfully and competently contribute?
- Are there adequate resources?
- Are the other collaborators solid?

Becoming a CollaborGREAT collaborator

If I can't answer yes to all four, I decline.

When you say yes, make it a full yes. That means clearing space. Making time. Showing up. It means collaborating like a professional – because you are one.

Protecting your time and energy

Collaboration takes time. Meetings, check-ins, co-creating deliverables, resolving misunderstandings, giving feedback – it all adds up. If you're not careful, collaboration can become the thing that keeps you from getting your other work done.

Here are a few ways to protect your energy:

- **Create 'deep work' windows**: Block time for solo focus.
- **Designate 'collaboration hours'**: That's when you respond, review or meet.
- **Watch out for tool overload**: A tech consultant told me, 'I was in six different platforms, just trying to keep track of which conversation was where.'
- **Audit your systems**: Some tools are helpful. Some are just bloat. Reduce unnecessary channels.

- **Speak up when collaboration goes sideways:** If someone's taking over, flaking out or dropping balls – name it. You don't need to assign blame. Just describe the behaviour and its impact.

Being a CollaborGREAT collaborator doesn't mean saying yes to everything. It means choosing wisely and then honouring those choices.

Collaboration beyond the office

The principles that support workplace collaboration also apply to life beyond the office. You're collaborating when you plan a vacation with friends, co-parent kids or organize a community event.

In these moments, you're managing interdependence, negotiating roles, setting expectations and aligning goals. You're also navigating emotions, power, logistics and time.

When I ask people to reflect on their most meaningful collaborative experiences, they don't just talk about work. They talk about shared dinners, community theatre, spiritual organizing, care teams for ageing parents and trips planned with friends. They talk about relationships, memories and mutual accomplishments.

Becoming a CollaborGREAT collaborator

Whether you're co-leading a workshop or planning a wedding, you're collaborating. You're negotiating shared purpose. Collaboration permeates how we live, how we explore, how we relate and even how we die.

CollaborGREAT expectations

Participating in deep collaborations amplifies your impact in the world. You will be amazed by how quickly you'll be able to make great things happen when you're engaged in CollaborGREAT relationships with high-performing people who know how to play well with others. The next step isn't to race out into the world to do lots of 'stuff' for the mere sake of doing stuff. Be choosy. Do the right constellation of stuff to advance your goals, whatever they may be.

Creating great collaborations matters because, well, *you* matter. Your *work* matters. Your *experience* of work matters. Your brilliance, your gifts, your wisdom, your talents, your abilities – collaboration can amplify *all* of these in a world brimming with both troubles to be fixed and opportunities to be realized.

Investing in the health of your collaborations and in your own development as a knowledgeable and effective collaborator not only increases your agency to get done what you want to get done, but it also helps others do the same. And, together, you all will make great things happen.

> ### ✎ So what? Over to you...
>
> 1. What questions can you ask yourself to help you decide when to say yes to collaboration?

Becoming a CollaborGREAT collaborator

2. What ideas are you eager to try to bring people together and facilitate collective action?

3. What's the next step for you in your professional (or personal) development when it comes to collaboration?

Day 10
Creating a culture of effective collaboration

Extraordinary collaboration doesn't happen by accident. It happens when individuals, teams and organizations commit to building environments where collaboration is supported, expected and rewarded.

Whether you're a team member or a leader, this is about how to create conditions where collaboration thrives – not just once, but over the long haul.

Start with culture

Culture is what people say and do without having to be asked. If we want to build a CollaborGREAT culture, we need to hardwire collaboration into how the organization functions.

Model healthy collaboration from the top. Culture is shaped by what leaders reward, what they tolerate and what they ignore. If you want collaboration, show collaboration.

Recognize and reward collaborative behaviours. Don't just reward outcomes – reward how people work together to get there. When someone goes out of their way to support a teammate, make that visible.

Make space for reflection. Ask people regularly about their collaborative experiences. What's working? What's not? What support would help?

Build time into the system. Collaboration takes time. If your workflows don't allow people time to talk, plan or reflect, collaboration becomes impossible.

And here's something I want you to really hear: You can't build a CollaborGREAT culture by just rolling out a new software tool or sending folks to a training session. You have to create structures, incentives and expectations that support healthy relational dynamics.

Otherwise, you're just layering process on top of dysfunction.

Creating a culture of effective collaboration

You don't need a fancy title to lead

Whether or not you're in a formal leadership role, you can shape collaborative culture. Influence happens sideways and from the middle, too.

Get curious about how people work best. Ask your teammates how they like to give and receive feedback, how they prefer to communicate and what they need to be successful.

Make the invisible visible. When you notice a pattern – good or bad – name it. 'Hey, I noticed that we've been cutting each other off in meetings. Can we try something different?'

Ask, 'What does success look like?' This question aligns everyone on the shared goal and helps clarify expectations.

Normalize reflection. You don't have to wait for a quarterly review cycle to reflect on how collaboration is going. You can say, 'How are we doing?' anytime.

And when someone collaborates in a way that's generous, thoughtful or effective – say something. Reinforce it. We often forget to acknowledge the good stuff, but that's how culture spreads.

People are talking. They're watching. And they're learning from each other.

Collaborate Better

Collaboration isn't a one-off

One of the most powerful things you can do is treat collaboration not as a fixed skill, but as something you're always learning.

Create feedback loops. Ask people to share what it's like to collaborate with you. If they're hesitant, that's data too.

Reflect on failed collaborations. What didn't work? What role did you play? What would you do differently next time?

Seek out models. Who are the CollaborGREATs around you? Watch them. Ask them questions. Learn from their habits.

Invest in development. Read books. Join workshops. Bring in facilitators. Collaboration is a muscle – you have to work it to build it.

The most CollaborGREAT teams I've worked with have rituals. They don't just do the work. They check in about how the work is going. They talk about relationships. They create space for realignment.

Systems matter

Collaboration doesn't happen in a vacuum. It happens within a system. And systems tend to give us exactly what they're designed to give us.

Creating a culture of effective collaboration

If collaboration is consistently going poorly, it might not be an individual problem. It might be a structural one.

That's why it's not enough to encourage individuals to be better collaborators. We have to shape the systems around them so that being a good collaborator is the path of least resistance.

Here's the point

Culture is shaped by what's modelled, rewarded and made possible. Leaders at all levels can cultivate CollaborGREAT dynamics through intentional choices and behaviours.

Collaboration must be supported not just in spirit but in structure – through time, tools and reinforcement.

Continuous reflection and development are essential to making collaboration a long-term strength, not just a one-off success.

So what? Over to you…

1. What collaboration are you currently part of that might benefit from a 'reset' conversation?

2. How can you build more regular celebration and reflection into your team's rhythm?

3. What personal habit could help you sustain your energy and engagement as a collaborator?

Conclusion

You've already taken a meaningful step in your development as a collaborator by spending time working through the ideas in this book. If your path is anything like mine, you will encounter new challenges and snags along the way as you enact the fine art of collaboration with new people, across novel contexts and on behalf of emerging problems. But now, with a bit of relationship science in your toolkit, at least your collaborative relationships will no longer be mysterious zones of confusion, tension and friction.

Every single one of the strategies in this book can be leveraged not only in the workplace, but also in your parenting, marriage and friendships. They're relevant to the dynamics unfolding at the co-op, community garden and place of worship. I invite you to grab hold of these ideas. Make them your own. Bring them to your many relationships, in the workplace and beyond.

Your collaborative know-how will create better relationships. Better relationships will create a more connected world. And a more connected world will create more care, curiosity and creativity.

This incredibly difficult collaboration stuff is so worth the effort.

So here's what I hope you take forward: a few new tools, a little more insight and a lot more permission to do collaboration on your terms – better, braver and more thoughtfully. Collaboration is never a one-time achievement. It's a daily choice, built moment by moment, conversation by conversation.

You don't have to wait for permission to start. You don't have to overhaul everything overnight.

You can begin right where you are – with the team you already have, the project you're already in, the relationships you're already part of.

Now go do something amazing. Together.

Endnotes

[1] Of the sample, 10% reported having 9 or more collaborations, with 6 people reporting 100 collaborations. And 10% of the sample reported generally having a large number of collaborators, ranging from 11 to 12,000. Gulp. Due to the anonymized nature of the survey, I was unable to reach out to ask clarifying follow-up questions.

[2] U.S. Bureau of Labor Statistics, (n.d.). Average hours per day spent in selected activities on days worked by employment status and sex, 2024 annual averages. Available from www.bls.gov/charts/american-time-use/activity-by-work.htm [accessed 24 April 2025].

[3] Simpli5, (n.d.). Organizational dynamics survey: Most businesses have a teamwork problem. Available from www.simpli5.com/resources/organizational-dynamics-survey-teamwork-problem/ [accessed 8 August 2022].

[4] E. Berscheid, M. Snyder and A. M. Omoto 'Measuring closeness: The relationship closeness inventory (RCI) revisited' in D. J. Mashek & A. P. Aron (eds), *Handbook of Closeness and Intimacy*. Lawrence Erlbaum Associates Publishers, 81–101 (2004).

[5] See www.debmashek.com/dl

Enjoyed this?
Then you'll love...

 *Collabor(h)ate: How to build incredible collaborative relationships at work (even if you'd rather work alone)* by Deb Mashek PhD

'We've all gotten stuck working with people we don't like. Thankfully, Deb Mashek has written a lively, actionable book to fix that. Combining her expertise as a psychologist and her experience as a consultant, she reveals how we can earn trust, repair relationships, and create collaborations that bring out the best in us.' – Adam Grant, #1 NYT bestselling author

Many people have mixed feelings about workplace collaboration. On the one hand, they know collaboration is essential to achieve complex goals. On the other hand, they know collaboration is a slog. People pull in different directions. There's desperately little communication and even less follow through. One person ends up doing all the work. The result? Friction mounts. Projects fizzle.

Enjoyed this? Then you'll love...

Great people walk. Here's why: very few of us ever receive any formal training in how to collaborate well. In *Collabor(h)ate*, Deb Mashek draws on her deep experience as a relationships researcher and collaboration facilitator to reveal everything you need to know to make workplace collaborations less painful and more productive. Dr Deb Mashek is an experienced business consultant, professor, higher education administrator and national nonprofit executive. She applies relationship science to help people collaborate better. Learn more at: www.collaborhate.com

Other 6-Minute Smarts titles

Building Great Teams (based on *Workshop Culture* by Alison Coward)

Customer Success Essentials (based on *The Customer Success Pioneer* by Kellie Lucas)

Do Change Better (based on *How to be a Change Superhero* by Lucinda Carney)

Find Your Confidence (based on *Coach Yourself Confident* by Julie Smith)

Get That Promotion (based on *Getting On* by Joanna Gaudoin)

How to be Happy at Work (based on *My Job Isn't Working!* by Michael Brown)

 *How to Get to Know Your Customer* (based on *Do Penguins Eat Peaches?* by Katie Tucker)

 *The Listening Leader* (based on *The Listening Shift* by Janie Van Hool)

 *Managing Big Teams* (based on *Big Teams* by Tony Llewellyn)

 *Mastering People Management* (based on *Mission: To Manage* by Marianne Page)

 *No-Nonsense PR* (based on *Hype Yourself* by Lucy Werner)

 Present Like a Pro (based on *Executive Presentations* by Jacqui Harper)

 *Reimagine Your Career* (based on *Work/Life Flywheel* by Ollie Henderson)

Sales Made Simple (based on *More Sales Please* by Sara Nasser Dalrymple)

The Speed Storytelling Toolkit (based on *Exposure* by Felicity Cowie)

Stay Focused (based on *Attention!* By Rob Hatch)

Write to Think (based on *Exploratory Writing* by Alison Jones)

Look out for more titles coming soon! Visit www.practicalinspiration.com for all our latest titles.

www.ingramcontent.com/pod-product-compliance
Lightning Source LLC
Chambersburg PA
CBHW020550030426
42337CB00013B/1030